Spirit of Springhill

Miners, Wives, Widows, Rescuers & Their Children Tell True Stories of Springhill's Coal Mining Disasters

By
Cheryl McKay

Purple PenWorks

SPIRIT OF SPRINGHILL

Front Cover Mining Grounds photo supplied by and used by
permission of the Springhill Heritage Museum.
Front Cover Miner's Hand photo by Christopher Price
Back Cover Miner's Pick & Tags photos by Cheryl McKay
Cover Design by Christopher Price

Interview segments & material used by permission of the
interview subjects.

To inquire about the rights to the screenplay, *Song of
Springhill*, contact the author: Cheryl@purplepenworks.com

Published in the United States of America
Copyright © 2014 by Cheryl McKay

ISBN 10: 0615990347
ISBN 13: 978-0615990347
2014 — First Edition

By Cheryl McKay

Song of Springhill (a love story)

Greetings from the Flipside a novel (with Rene Gutteridge)
Never the Bride a novel (with Rene Gutteridge)
Finally the Bride: Finding Hope While Waiting
Finally Fearless: How Overcoming Anxiety Helped Me Find True Love
The Ultimate Gift (screenplay)
The Ultimate Life (screen story)
Gigi: God's Little Princess DVD (screenplay)
Wild & Wacky, Totally True Bible Stories Series (with Frank Peretti)

Dedication:
For Charles McKay
"Dado"
My grandfather who survived the 1958 Bump in
the Springhill, Nova Scotia coal mines.

For those who
keep hope alive
in the midst of great adversity

TABLE OF CONTENTS

Springhill's Story in the 1950s.. 8

The Interviews

Disaster Survivors:
Caleb Rushton...15
Herb Pepperdine...23
Ken Melanson...26

Family Members of Survivors:
Tom "Tommy" McKay...30
Joyce (McKay) Harroun...39
Debbie Betty-Brazie..50
Norma Ruddick..55
Valerie Ruddick MacDonald...61

Rescuers / Family of Rescuers:
Bill Booth...72
Ken Warren...75
Dr. Arnold Burden..78

Children of Victims:
Jerry Gillis..89
Jack & Keith Bourgeois..92
Valarie Tabor Alderson..99
Ethel Fisher Gilbert...112

Ripple Effect of Life..118

About *Song of Springhill: a love story*...............127

About the Author....................................130

Springhill's Story in the 1950s

Spirit of Springhill is more than just a book of interviews; it's a record of a legacy. It's a tribute to the people of a small town in Nova Scotia, Canada: those who died, those who survived, those left behind, and the heroes who worked tirelessly to save people's lives. Springhill has been a town that has endured many tragedies, yet it's also a place to find inspiration in the ways it has bounced back from adversity.

Ironically, as I was nearing publication of this book (in 2014), Springhill received news that it was losing its township status after 125 years of being an independent town. Every person I spoke to about this was clear:

You can't take Springhill out of the Springhiller.

The people of this town are proud of their heritage, which for most goes back many generations. Springhillers know their parents' stories, their grandparents' stories, and the stories of many of their ancestors.

My journey to tell the story of Springhill started in 2001. As a screenwriter, I believe there should be a movie that shows the disasters, followed by the astounding miracle rescues that happened in this town. My dad had often told me he thought the story would be worth telling in a movie; he was right. I found a town plagued with great tragedy, but also, astounding miracles. The resulting screenplay is what was used to develop the novel version, *Song of Springhill: a love story.*

The miracles blew me away. If I made this story up in a screenplay, you would find it tough to believe. But it happened!

During such tragic events—long after loved ones thought their men had died underground— large pockets of men would be found alive. This didn't just happen once. It happened during the 1956 Explosion (where a pocket of 50 men were found days after the disaster), and in 1958 when two groups of men were found. Twelve men were found six days after the Bump, and yet another set of miners was found eight and a half days after the Bump. Seven men came out of the No. 2 mine alive that day—to the cheers and delight of the town that had feared they were gone forever.

What captured my heart the most in digging into the stories of this mining town was the close-knit camaraderie that existed among the men, and their loyalty to one another. True friendship forever tied them together. Then there were the women of Springhill—ones who displayed an unwavering strength in the midst of the unknown, sometimes displaying an inexplicable faith.

To research for writing the script in 2001, I started interviewing survivors, widows, kids of the victims, children of survivors, rescuers, other mine workers, doctors, engineers—anyone who would talk to me about what happened in this town in the 1950s. I ended up with this collection of interviews that tells the behind-the-scenes stories of what went into the fictional version, as told through the screenplay and novel, *Song of Springhill: a love story.*

These pages hold stories narrated directly by the people themselves, some of which have passed away since I interviewed them. I'm honored to have preserved this little piece of history in their words and in their honor. There are so many heroes among the good people of Springhill.

My grandfather, Charles Hugh McKay—also known as "Dado" to his grandchildren—died when I was fifteen years old. I wish when I were younger, I had been more interested in asking him questions about his life as a miner, and the miracles that spared his life. It wasn't something he voluntarily talked about when not asked. Years after he passed away, I embarked on a quest to get to know more about what his life was like. His check tag number was #712 just like the one my father's hand holds on the cover of this book.

It was several key pieces from my grandfather's life that served as the inspiration for the story, regarding his involvement in both the 1956 Explosion and the 1958 Bump.

My aunt, Joyce Harroun, was the first to share with me his story relating to the 1956 Explosion. She said my grandfather switched shifts that day with another man and got off work just a couple hours before the mine blew up.

This meant that my grandfather's life was spared, but the man who switched shifts with him died. If my grandfather had gone to work at his normal time that day, he would have died for sure. I never would have met him. It also meant that the team of men my grandfather was used to working with died that day too; he lost a lot of his friends. It was the only time my aunt ever saw my grandfather cry up until that point in his life.

I went on a quest to discover who this person was who died in my grandfather's place. You will get to read about him later in this collection of interviews, as I was able to find that answer.

In 1958, my grandfather was trapped underground when The Bump hit, which was one of the biggest disasters in coal mining history. It was also the deepest coal mine in North America at the time.

In this book, you will hear about the three tragedies that struck Springhill in the 1950s: the 1956 Explosion, the 1957 Main Street Fire, and the 1958 Bump.

I am forever grateful to all of those who allowed me to talk to them about these events, and for their permission to use their stories. I hope you enjoy reading about what these beloved people shared with me.

I do hope through this book of interviews and the fictional novel, I've captured the heart of this beloved town and its refusal to give up on its own, its refusal to surrender hope in the midst of the direst of circumstances.

Springhill, you inspire me. Current town or not, I hope your unquenchable spirit continues to inspire others by letting your story live on.

You show us that miracles do happen.

Cheryl McKay (Book Author)

The Interviews

The majority of the interviews are written in a Q&A format, in the interview subjects' own words. If they handwrote or typed these surveys, I preserved the Canadian spellings they used. The interviews that are not Q&A style were most likely conducted in person. It's an honor, after over a decade, to finally share these stories. (Please Note: most of the photos are decades old so the resolution will be low.)

Disaster

Survivors

Caleb Rushton
Survivor of the 1958 Bump
(Interviewed July 2001)

1. What was the daily routine, working in the mines, from start to finish? Describe a normal day at work.

Normally, men went to the Wash House from their homes. They would change from street clothes into their mining clothes. Then they went to the Lamp Cabin, handing in a check number for which they received a battery-operated lamp. Then they waited for the trolleys to take them down in the mines. When they got off the trolleys, they walked into the actual work places. Miners dug the coal. Labourers did various jobs. As a miner, you had to have papers to dig coal. Papers weren't required by the ones who did the labour work. At the end of the shift, all would walk out to the trolleys and return to the surface. They turned in their lamps and retrieved their check numbers then went to the Wash House where they would shower, put street clothes on, and go to their homes.

2. What was the work itself like? Did your job responsibilities rotate?

The work itself was quite hard, digging coal, lifting heavy timbers, shoveling stone. Job responsibilities didn't change or rotate unless a person got to do a different job. He might request a different job or his boss could get him another job. Ordinarily, you were stuck with the job you were given upon being hired.

3. What was the procedure for the shifts and shift changes? How often did you change the shift you'd be working?

When you started in the mines, you were put in jobs that required help or extra help. Mostly these jobs were kept for various periods, depending on whether men were off on compensation or had decided the work wasn't for them. This gave someone else a chance to get a particular job. There were three shifts a day. 11pm to 7am, 7am to 3pm, and 3pm to 11pm. The work week was Monday to Friday so you changed weekly, on Mondays. The 11pm-7am shift was a maintenance shift. The 11pm shift was worked by men who preferred this type of work or that shift.

4. What would you have done for work if you weren't a coal miner? What were the options back then?

The types of work available at that time were a store clerk, truck driver, logging work in the sawmill, janitor work. The turnover in these jobs was very little, and the mines paid the highest wages for the area.

5. What was the pay scale for a miner? What kind of lifestyle could a miner afford?
Miners were paid on a contract basis, so much for a ton of coal dug. At the time, miners could get as much as $15.00 plus or minus for a shift, whereas labourers only received $10 a shift. A miner of that day could have a moderate lifestyle. They weren't rich but comfortable.

6. Did you rotate which team of men you worked with? Or did you usually work with the same men?
I worked with the same men.

7. Where were you during the 1956 Explosion?
At the time of the Explosion, I had been working in the Lamp Cabin as a repairman. I was on a steady 7am-3pm shift. I had gone home, and we had just sat down to eat when we heard the bang.

8. Before the Bump, what was the attitude of the miners about working in the No. 2 mine? Did they feel like they were in danger?

Before the Bump, a lot of older miners said that there would be a serious bump if they brought the walls out together. They felt they were in great danger. The mine manager was only taking orders from the people above him. None of it was his fault. The mining union and board members told the company not to line up the walls. But they kept using that method anyway. The new method did not increase production. Most of us just wanted to keep our jobs, so we kept quiet.

9. You are considered one of the "Miracle Survivors" of the Bump. When they thought everyone had perished underground, you were found with a group of men six days later. Talk about those days you spent underground. What was it like, and what did you do to survive?

During the six days underground, we slept and talked. Our lights only lasted a couple of days, if that, so we could not move around that much. During the night of the Bump and the next day, we looked for ways of escape, but there were none. We didn't have the tools or the energy to dig our way out. Interaction was normal under the circumstances. We talked about our families, friends, told stories, had a few laughs. I really think sleep took a lot of our time, and we didn't realize we were sleeping. I know this was true in my own case. I had a wristwatch with a luminous dial so I could keep track of time.

10. What was the biggest struggle for each man stuck underground?

The biggest struggle for the men in our group was not being able to get out and not knowing when we would.

11. How was your relationship with your fellow twelve miners before the Bump vs. after the Bump?

My relationship with the men of our group was always friendly, as we had known each other for years. That friendly feeling prevailed after the Bump also.

12. Describe how you were rescued? How did the rescue workers get to you, and what happened as soon as they got you out?

We were rescued because barefaced miners toiled selflessly to dig through about 200 feet of coal to get to us. They had to put the coal in buckets and pass it back between their legs to the next fellow in line. Their workspace was only three feet wide and three feet high. Then they lugged us out on stretchers to the trolleys. No easy task! We were taken directly to All Saint's Hospital and given tests for a couple of days.

13. What was your recovery like?
I recovered quite quickly, but was unable to work for a couple months.

14. Did you ever go back into a mine after the Bump?
I never returned to the mines after that. They actually stopped paying us the moment the mine bumped and didn't pay us for all the time we were stuck underground.

15. Explain what it was like living in Springhill: town life, church life, the people, entertainment.
At the time of the Bump, Springhill was a quiet little town of 7000. Now it's roughly 4000 (in 2001). People were friendly. Mining brings out a closeness you don't see in other places. Church life was good and we attended weekly. As I said, people were friendly and always willing to help one another. We had a bowling alley, a movie theater, Fraternal Lodge, and Service Clubs. Many variety concerts took place in the theater.

16. What do you know about my grandfather's rescue (Charles McKay)?
After the Bump, your grandfather walked most of the way out, up the west side of the back slope. It was an auxiliary slope where the haulage equipment was, where miners got in the cars to

ride up and down the mine, the same one they'd used to move the coal out by swapping the cars. It was not in the heat of the Bump. It still had damage, and they would have felt it. But it wasn't nearly the same damage where my group was trapped.

Author's Note: I had a chance to talk to Caleb's wife, Pat, about what this time was like for her. Pat said, "I had been working at the church that day, met my mother in the street, and went to the mines. I went to the mines until the first people came out. It was like a dream, crazy with people coming and going. People were everywhere, like reporters. I waited at the first aid station outside the mines." Pat said the whole time they were waiting for word on whether Caleb was alive or not, she never felt like she could say he was gone. She didn't want to think one way or the other until she had confirmation.

In Loving Memory
Caleb Rushton
(January 16, 1923-June 10, 2008)

Cheryl, Caleb & Pat Rushton (2001)

Herb Pepperdine
Survivor of the 1958 Bump
(Interviewed July 2001)

1. What was your job in the mines?

You could get miner's papers by working a couple of years first in the mines. Then you could take an oral exam, about what to do and not to do. Labourers would build supports for the roof, run trips, build stone packs. As labourers, we worked with miners, not separate. We would fill 24 coal boxes on one trip up. Twenty-two men would work together and all get the same pay. For example, when 22 miners were on the wall, the labourers, two sets of two men would be on the bottom and top building stone packs.

2. Were you working the day of the Explosion?

I was not involved in the Explosion, since that was in the No. 4. I was working in the No. 2 during the Explosion but on day shift, building supports for the roof. So, I wasn't around.

3. Tell us about working in the No. 2 during the Bump:

We had an early bump that day and shut everything down. It was really quiet down there. The problem was in lining walls up. The miners knew there'd be trouble. [The company] in Cape Breton decided to do this method, to try to stop bumps. It didn't work. The union was concerned too. It wasn't about greed. They didn't get more production out of it.

The No. 2 used the retreat wall system— drove the levels on the way in and extract the coal on the way out. The No. 4 was advance wall. If walls had been staggered in the No. 2, the Bump would have happened at the 13,400 level and no others. It wouldn't have affected the other walls. But it did because they had lined them up. That made it worse.

It ended up being a big mess underground. People, good people, my best friends, we were stuck down there together. We celebrated Garnie Clarke's twenty-ninth birthday underground and sang to him. We ate a chocolate bar that I found in someone else's lunch. We also tried to eat an egg sandwich, but it had gone bad.

After a while, I really thought it was over. And then, they found us.

4. What was your rescue like?
I was put on stretcher to be rescued and carried out. At the time of the rescue, I was lying in there

and saw lights. Then I was in All Saints Hospital for one week. Once I got out, I saw they had paid me for six hours the day of the Bump. The company didn't take responsibility. They packed up and walked out of town.

5. Did you work as a coal miner after the rescue?
I worked in a syndicate mine for ten more years.

Cheryl, Herb Pepperdine (2001)

Ken Melanson
Survivor of the 1956 Explosion
(Interviewed July 2001, while he was the Underground Supervisor at the Springhill Miner's Museum)

1. Were you worried about safety as a miner?

I wasn't afraid of the mines. I wanted to work there because of the better pay. It was $10 a day instead of $4-6 in other jobs. I felt like Harold Gordon (Mine Manager) was a smart man. The engineers plus other board people and Gordon had to make decisions on mining practices. He couldn't have decided that alone. He was a man doing his job.

Before the Bump, there were complaints about safety. Many said, "The big one is coming." There was too much stress down there. They thought it would happen. The coal face was tight, hard to dig. Sometimes that indicates a bump is coming. Staggering the walls was the norm, but they lined up the walls.

Harry Terris (the board member and head of the union) was on the side of the miners who felt it was unsafe. Before the blow up in the No. 4, we had been having problems all that week. We may have even had a small fire. The first shift had to work with gas that week.

2. Talk about the day of the 1956 Explosion:

I was 19 years old. I was with two friends at the Miner's Hall right before the Explosion. We hung out, then went to work. Neither of my friends came out alive.

When I arrived at the mines, I went to the Wash House, then the Lamp Cabin, then inside the mine to the 5400 level. At 5:07 p.m., a coal car jumped the track and cut the electric cable. I was inside mine from Thursday to Monday morn. It felt like the other side of Hell. I didn't think we'd get out. We had no food or water.

I was with Con Embree's group of fifty men. We created a barricade for the gas, to block it. We cut notches in the pipe to breathe through. We were very scared, especially once we saw cement in the water that flowed into mine. That meant they used cement to seal the mine. We felt like this meant no one thought anyone was alive, so they had sealed the mine to stop the fires. Yet we were alive and trapped.

We found out later Harold Gordon had told everyone that it was unlikely anyone was alive. On Sunday, Con Embree seemed to feel it was over. He asked if anyone wanted to write last entries in the journal that people would find later. We wrote goodbyes.

3. How were you finally rescued?

The rescuers made their way through the auxiliary air slope, barefaced, some of them. Once they found Charlie Burton, the first guy who made it to the surface alive, he told them there were many others alive down there at the 5400 level. Word spread through town with great excitement. We were told not to move—help was on the way. Sadly, Charlie Burton, who survived the Explosion, was killed, two years later, in the Bump. Once rescued, I got paid one hour of pay for all the time I was in the mine.

4. What do you know about my grandfather's story, related to the day of the Explosion? We understand he switched shifts for someone that day and that man was killed instead. We are trying to find out who that may have been.

Lester Fisher and Gerald Dawson are two men who did the same job as your grandfather. Either one may be who took his shift that day. Both of them died.

I liked working with your grandfather, Charlie. Sometimes we'd finish our tasks before our shift was over. He was nice and let us ride up to the top before the shift was done.

Family Members of Survivors

Tom "Tommy" McKay
Son of Charles Hugh McKay — Survivor of the 1958 Bump
(Interviewed February 2013)

1. What was it like growing up in Springhill?
While there were some bad things that happened there, life was simple and fun and you had good friends. You never felt insecure or in danger. Kids today, you can't let them do what we did, like being allowed to leave in the morning and not come home until dinner. We were able to go out and hang with buddies, go exploring in the woods. It wasn't dangerous. Mothers never had to worry about their kids. Whoever's house you were near when out playing at lunchtime, his mother would feed you. I went to church, Boy Scouts, played youth hockey. The simplicity of life in Springhill is what stands out.

As you got to your teen years, you went to dances. Like most boys, we were afraid to ask girls to dance. I went to dances at the Miner's Hall and at the Armory.

The grocery store would trust a miner to pay for food later when he got paid. They'd let you take a bag of food and put it on a tab. I remember going to the store to pick up things and my parents would pay after payday. During mine closures, the grocery store would carry people until the mines were working again.

2. Describe Springhill in terms of a mining town.
It was the industry of the town; the people of the town worked there. You didn't think of it as living in a mining town.

Today, people don't have as much pride about where they live, but I liked living in Springhill. We felt pride about being part of something. We were living in a world before a lot of television and media coverage. So we didn't realize, being there, how the rest of the world lived. We weren't comparing ourselves to other towns. I do remember going to Boston and seeing how big everything was, how much traffic they had, the trolley, a lot of people, and seeing a different way of life.

3. Talk about having a father who was a coal miner. What was that like? Did you worry?
The only time I thought about it is if something, like an accident, happened at the mine. Most times, I didn't really give it a thought. I was young. Around 1954, I started hearing about people dying or getting hurt. I would hear about

other people's fathers, and I'd realize my father worked in a place that wasn't always safe. But I didn't think a whole lot about it. When something went wrong in the mines, the first thing I would think was, "Is my father working right now?" It wasn't until later on in life, I reflected back on how he was in danger every day of his life there, just like he was on October 23, 1958, during the Bump. I did sometimes feel envious if a friend had a father who worked above ground because I knew his father was safer. For example, some fathers worked in the hoist house that pulled the cars out of the mine. It seemed safer. Except in the 1956 Explosion, some of the bankhead workers were killed, and it turned out to not always be safe. My dad never talked about working there and never seemed to express a fear of being there. If he felt it, he didn't say it.

4. Did you ever want to be a coal miner, to follow in your father's footsteps? Did you ever think you would have to out of necessity?
I never thought I was going to be a coal miner. I had no idea what I was going to do, but I knew it wouldn't be that. Later on, out of curiosity, I probably would like to have worked in a coal mine for one week, during normal shifts, just so I'd know what he did. You can never really imagine it; you have to experience it. I believe I

would probably have been petrified, but maybe not. In Springhill, they wouldn't let you take your kid to work with you. If I had lived in that town another five years, I would've had to make the choice of whether or not I would work there.

5. How was your mother affected by having a husband who was a coal miner?

She worried about a lot of things in general. So I imagine she was nervous about him being there. When they moved us out of Springhill after The Bump, my mom got a job for the first time in her life and became a nurse. She seemed to be much happier. I wonder if it was partly because she no longer had to worry about Dad.

6. What did your father tell you about the mining accident he had that put him in the hospital before you were born?

He was hit by a coal box, and it crushed his pelvis. It took a long time to recover. It was around the Second World War. He ended up in the hospital for quite a while. I believe that's what kept him from joining the Army. A lot of people went into armed services from Springhill during that war.

7. Where were you when the 1956 Explosion happened, and what did you do?

I had just delivered my last newspaper for the

day, the Springhill Record. I was with a friend, Doug Russell. Our mothers were close friends. We were on Lisgar Street, in perfect eyeshot to see the Explosion at the mines below. We were on the sidewalk, on our bikes. We felt the ground shake, turned around and saw a big ball of fire shoot up in the air. It was like watching a bomb go off. Flames shot hundreds of feet into the air. I quickly thought of my father, "Is Dad working right now?" My mental process was that he wasn't there that morning when I went to school, which meant today he was on day shift. Dayshift was now over. I knew based on what time it was, he wouldn't be underground because the shift would have changed. You're selfishly hoping it's not your dad underground. You first think of your own father, but that's human nature. Then your thoughts move to other people's fathers who might be working that day. I knew fathers of my friends worked there.

I went home after the Explosion, but my dad had already left the house to check on what was happening at the mine. I spent a little bit of time out at the mines after the Explosion. Everyone in town migrated over there.

They made us go back to school during the search and rescue operation over the next few days so we wouldn't be in the way. After the Explosion, the only time my father went back in the No. 4 mine was to be a part of the crew that had to recover the bodies of the fallen miners. My dad didn't talk about that at all; we just knew he had to do it.

8. Where were you when the 1957 Main Street Fire broke out? Did you go to the scene?

It was December 26, Boxing Day and the day after Christmas. It was evening. We were still awake, watching TV. In Springhill, we knew there was a fire because they blew whistles. Plus we could tell where the fire was by how many whistles we heard.

My dad and I went to see what was burning. We went over to Main Street and watched the fire from the steps of Saffron's store. The fire spread and that store was gone by the next morning. Later into the evening, we watched the fire from the window of our house on Maple Street. There were a whole bunch of burned out buildings by the next day. It burned out Main Street on both sides and took out some houses on Fir Street, near where we used to live.

9. Where were you when the 1958 Bump happened? Did you go to the mines?

When the Bump happened, I had just left Dawson's Pool Room above Dawson's Groceries, on Junction Road near Main Street. I was on the sidewalk in front of the place, about to go home. The earth shook. I immediately knew this time my dad was working. I went straight to the mine.

I was in the Lamp Cabin waiting for news with many other people. Word came that miners were coming out of the mine, but they didn't say who. And then my dad came through the door of the Lamp Cabin. I was the first person he saw. He wasn't hurt and told me, "Go home and tell your mother that you saw me. She won't believe anybody else." He needed to get cleaned up before he went home.

When I got home, the house was full of people. Relatives were there from Amherst waiting for news. I told them he was out of the mines. They were obviously very happy. My father came home shortly after.

10. How did your father react once he was rescued? Did he want to go back underground?
He was happy he was home but sad many others didn't make it. The mine company's future was uncertain at the time, whether or not they could stay open because they'd sustained so much damage. He'd had a lot of close calls too. His sisters had been trying to get him to move to Boston since after the 1956 Explosion. Every time we visited them down there, they'd talk to him about moving there. After the Bump, they realized

there probably wouldn't be much of a coal mine industry. He had a standing job offer in Boston, by someone who knew his sisters, to work for a wholesale egg company. His sister, my Aunt Leona, had already lined this up for him, if he was ever willing to leave Springhill. My dad's other sister, Jen, had come to Springhill as soon as she heard about the Bump, and my father went back to Boston with her to see about the job my other aunt had set up. They left before they found the second group of miners in the second miracle rescue. They heard about that rescue on the radio.

He came back to Springhill a week later and already had the job and announced we were moving. He had wanted to be in Springhill with his mother, but he took the job. He was interviewed in a Boston paper while he was visiting there. The whole world was searching for stories at the time about Springhill, and since he was one of those 174 people stuck underground, they wanted to talk to him about what it was like.

If the Bump hadn't happened, we never would have moved. He felt it was necessary to take care of the family. My parents moved in January 1959. I joined them a bit later. He lived in that little town for over forty years of his life; moving was a tough choice for him. Out of necessity, a lot of people had to move. He had worked in the mines since he was fifteen, for about twenty-seven years.

Cheryl & her Dad (Tom McKay) (2013)

Cheryl & her Dad (Tom McKay) (2011)

Joyce (McKay) Harroun
Daughter of Charles McKay — Survivor of the 1958 Bump
(Interviewed in 2001 & 2014)

Author's Note: Joyce is my aunt (my dad's sister), so her references to Dad or Mom are to my grandfather and grandmother, Charlie & Ethel McKay. In researching to write the script and novel, I wanted a clear picture of what it was like to grow up in this small town back in that time period. My aunt colored in the most detailed picture of this setting, which helped me paint in details for the fictional story. Enjoy the little walk back in time:

1. Share about this town you grew up in and what you did for fun:
Springhill was a great place to be a child and grow up. Summers were long and hot. As children, we always played outdoors.

Behind my grandmother and grandfather's house (Ma and Pa McKay) on Maple Street, there was an old garage full of old wood and mud floors. It was dirty. As a group of kids, Keith

Wilson, Juddy Anderson, Jimmie Weatherbee, Jean Megeney (my cousin) and myself and any other brothers or sisters we could drum up made a clubhouse out of the old garage. We met daily. If you had a penny, you brought it and saved for a fund to send to the war. World War II was on at this time. After the meeting, we used some of our collection of pennies at Fox's Store at the bottom of Maple Street for penny candy.

As winter came, we would go coasting behind my Uncle Marvin's house on Maple Street down backfields to North Street.

On Friday nights, Pa McKay, who worked for the liquor store on Main Street, would come home with a large tub of ice cream. We were told that each Friday, we could bring all the kids to Ma & Pa's kitchen and sun porch and Ma would give each of us a large bowl of ice cream. It all had to be eaten, as she only had a small icebox for refrigeration.

During these years, Dad would always take me with him to ballgames in the park on lower Main Street. They'd sometimes close the mines during the playoffs games for the Fencebusters. It was a series with all Nova Scotia teams.

The Hollywood Dare Devils came once a year to perform tricks with the cars on the racetrack surrounding the ball field. They also had racehorses and races on the track.

We also played War with wooden guns, and we'd play Kick the Can.

We skated 2 to 3 times a week at the Arena and went to movies at the Capital Theater. We all had bicycles. We learned to make kites and fly them, and colored Easter eggs. We went to the Hot Dog Stand on Main Street.

Our house was always open to my friends, including for sleepovers. But if the girls got homesick at night, Dad would get dressed and walk them home. (Remember: we had no car!)

Growing up in Springhill was wonderful, as there was a lot to do.

2. What was available in terms of the arts, music, and dancing back then?

I started tap dancing when I was 7 or 8 years old, taught on Saturday mornings in the Capital Theater by Girlie Mason (Brown). For many years she taught about 12 girls. This was free of charge, but you had to be there every Saturday. No excuses! We never missed it, as it was enjoyable.

We danced in several Minstrel Shows that Girlie put on each year with the End men (faces colored black). We'd have a large chorus line of men. The tap dancers usually did one or two numbers at this performance. I stayed with this group of girls until I was 16 years old.

We'd also have school plays at Christmas

time.

Around 1948, Jim and Jean Gogan opened the "Avalon" on lower Main Street. It was a dance hall that had a lunch counter and a jukebox. Here, we learned to dance. It was open Friday night, Saturday afternoon and evening. It cost ten cents to get in, five cents to play the jukebox. When we ran out of nickels, Jim would turn the jukebox on automatic so we could still dance. (This is where I met Gerald in 1951, got married in 1953, and we had our 60 year anniversary in 2013.)

On my fourteenth birthday, Mom and Dad paid to take my friends to the Avalon and then we went back to our small house for lunch after. We gathered up more friends than planned! They all wanted to dance, so Dad rolled up my Grandmother Tooke's Persian rug on the living room floor. The piano was played and we danced. The phone was ringing at midnight with parents looking for their kids. Dad saw to it that they all got home safely. What a party to remember!

Also in Springhill, the different groups or lodges held balls, which were formal dances where women wore long gowns and the men wore suits, shirts, and ties. An orchestra called the "Acadians" played for these. I got my first formal gown at 16, and went with Gerald to the Miner's Hall for one of these dances. Oh, it was elegant! If a ball happened to be at Mason's Ball, Gerald's grandparents, Mame and Roach McKay led the grand march, which they always had at the start of the dances.

I took piano lessons from Gladys McPherson. Everyone took music lessons. All parents thought kids had to take it, but the boys hated it. We'd have a concert at the end of the season.

Prior to taking these lessons, Dad taught me to play the piano when I was a little girl. He played by ear. I could play chords and melody, and he and I would play duets on the piano. Old time music. When I started taking lessons and reading music, I found it very hard. Miss McPherson would get quite upset with me, trying to keep me on track.

Dad's mother, Ma McKay, had a piano in her living room, and that's where we would spend many hours having fun. Jean Megeney, my cousin, was also taking lessons. We would play duets on the piano. Our grandmother, Ma, put up with a lot from us!

3. What kinds of vacations did you take?

Mom and Dad always rented a cottage every year for two weeks for the miner's vacation. We didn't have a car but a friend of Dad's with a truck would arrive and pick us up with bedding, groceries and cart us off to Heathers Beach for two weeks. At the end of vacation, he would come back and pick us up. I can still hear Mom and Dad playing cards out in the kitchen / living room by an oil lamp with neighbors or friends. Their laughter was great. As kids, we'd lie in bed and listen.

Outside of the two-week vacation, we could go to Heathers Beach on Sunday in the back of Herb Boss's truck for fifty cents. He had a large truck with wooden benches on both sides, open to the sky but a gate put across the back so we wouldn't fall out.

Ma and Pa McKay would go on trips to the United States, with Pa's brother Lawrence and Eva McKay. They would always bring back big gifts to Jean and myself. I still have my talking doll they brought to us when we were four years old. We both lived with Ma & Pa on Maple Street until I was five years old, and Jean was twelve. Three generations and two babies born in 1936 all lived in the house on Maple Street.

4. What was school like in Springhill?

Going to school was good. Our school had no gym so we didn't have basketball or gym sports. Our exercise was walking to and from school. (No school busses for town kids!)

High School was always busy. We had male and female teachers. The principal taught geometry. We had history, science, French,

English, Geography, Latin, Biology, Music, and Drama.

5. Describe Main Street, as you remember it, before the 1957 Fire:
Main Street was lined with stores: clothing, jewelry, shoes, hardware, a hat shop. (Everyone wore hats to church on Sunday.) Grocery stores, drugstores, doctor's office, churches. Churches were filled to capacity in those days. You arrived early to get a seat. They had Sunday School, youth groups, and picnics. No one said on Sunday morning, "I'm not going to church." We enjoyed it.

6. Tell me what you remember about your father's experiences during the 1956 Explosion:
The disasters were terrible. Dad was not working for the first one in 1956. So we knew he was safe. He had switched shifts with someone else that day, or he would have been underground.

Young men in their twenties were killed. Neighbor boys and boys we hung around with during our early and teen years died.

In 1956, the people my father (your grandfather) worked with for years were killed. He cried. He was so broken up because his friends were killed.

It was standard to have people killed in the

mines, but when it was people you knew or went to school with or your friend's fathers, it got very tough. In 1954, my best friend, Olwyn Hunter's, father, Wesley, was killed in the mines—along with four other men—and I suffered along with her.

7. What do you remember about the 1958 Bump?
When Dad got switched to No. 2, there was a lot of pressure there. He didn't like it. He would have nosebleeds because the mine was so deep.

The day of the Bump, Dad was down at the bottom of the mines, and it destroyed part of the mines was above him. The only way for these men to get out was to walk around and up. Of course on the bank head, no one knew if they were alive or not.

While Tommy (your dad) waited at the mine, I stayed on Maple Street with Mom and Ma McKay. Mom's sisters and their husbands had arrived from Amherst to wait for news. Dad always had white hair, but when he came through the door, his hair was even whiter. His first remarks were that he would never go down in the mines gain. He never did and the mine never reopened.

Joyce (McKay) & Gerald Harroun (2001)

Cheryl, Tom, Denise, Joyce, Gerald, Heather
(McKay) Gebbia & Chris Gebbia (2003)

"Dado" teaching Cheryl to play the organ

Cheryl, Joyce, Charlie "Dado" McKay, Ethel
(Tooke) McKay

Joyce & Tommy

Tommy & their mom (Ethel)

Debbie Betty-Brazie
Step-Daughter of Charles McKay — Survivor of the 1958 Bump
(Interviewed in 2014)

Author's Note: Debbie was my step-aunt, after my grandfather married her mother, years after my grandmother, Ethel (Tooke) McKay, passed away. Debbie used to spend time asking my grandfather a lot of questions about his years as a miner. I interviewed her to see what she remembered about the stories he told her regarding the two disasters. As mentioned, the grandkids all called him "Dado."

1. What did Dado share with you about Springhill?

He shared that Springhill was a very small town with a close-knit community, where everyone knew everyone else. Most men worked in the coal mines.

Dado was extremely proud of Springhill and loved to tell us stories of his mining days, the disasters he had experienced, and how those disasters shaped his life and his family.

2. Did he mention being afraid to go underground?

He said, "I didn't have the good sense to be afraid. I just knew what I had to do, and I did it."

3. What did he share with you about the 1956 disaster?

Dado swapped that day to a day shift so he had just left the mine when the Explosion happened. I do remember him saying he would have been in the mine if he had not swapped shifts.

While Dado was not in the mine when the Explosion happened, many of his friends were. He told the story of how he had finished his shift and had returned home. He was sitting in the living room reading the newspaper when he heard the windows rattle, and then the sound of the Explosion. (He said he could feel it hit first, then heard it.) He put his newspaper down, got up from his chair, grabbed his coat and hat and left the house. He knew what had just happened. No one had to tell him. He and all the other miners who weren't underground went directly to the mine to help.

4. What did he share with you about the 1958 Bump?

He said the longer you worked in the mines, the closer you were to being involved in a mining accident. Dado was in the mine this day working his shift. He said it was the worst bump in the history of North America at the time.

Dado explained that a "bump" is when the ceiling of the mine collapses in and the floor of the mine heaves up. He was working close to some sort of large machinery, and it was that machinery that saved his life and prevented him from getting crushed.

Dado said he and other men working in that area of the mine that were not killed or injured in the Bump began their journey to the surface, walking, assisting or carrying injured miners with them.

The mine was pitch-black. The only light the men had were the lamps on their helmets. They knew they needed to get out as quickly as possible, as poisonous gasses would be filling the mine. Dado said he went by many co-workers who were trapped, injured or already dead. It was so dark they could hardly see. Sometimes, they just knew or sensed they were passing by men who were already dead but couldn't see them.

They could hear other men calling for help. They helped those men that they could get to, but most of the injured were trapped.

They made a map of each location where they believed men were trapped to give to the draegermen who could rescue them.

Dado said it took them many hours to get to the surface on foot. He was not sure how much time had elapsed.

It was the middle of the night when they emerged from the mine, and Dado said there were cheers from the crowds that had gathered when the men appeared. He thought the entire town was there! It was a confusing moment for him.

The group of men Dado walked to the surface with was one of the last groups of survivors to come out of the mine (before the miracle rescues from six and eight days later).

5. What did he share with you about what it was like to see the face of my father once he was safely out of the mines?

The way he explained it, that moment was one of those "life changing" moments. His eyes found your dad, Tom, waiting for his father to come out of the mine. Dado said it was at that instant he realized, looking into Tom's face and seeing his son's expression, the true gravity of the situation and that he would never go back into the mines again.

The mine closed following the Bump, and the economy of Springhill fell into ruin as the mines had been the main employment in town. With the mines closed, there was no work. Many families were forced to leave Springhill. Dado moved your grandmother (Ethel) and your dad to the United States to the Boston area.

So, if the Bump had never taken place, your dad would not have moved to the States. He would not have met your mother, and you and your sister, Heather, would not have been born.

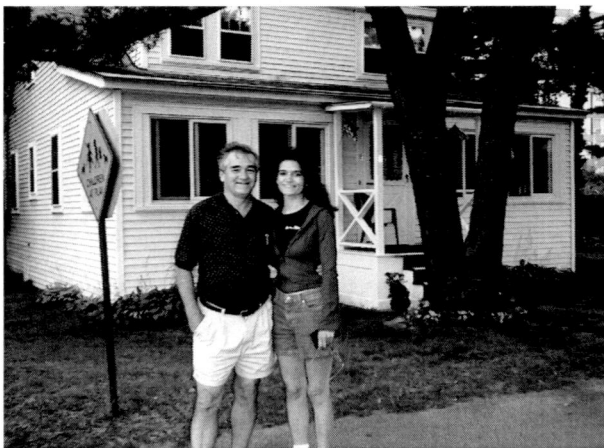

Tom McKay & Cheryl in front of the home where Charles McKay lived in Old Orchard Beach, ME with Debbie Betty-Brazie's mother, Ella

Norma Ruddick
Wife of Maurice Ruddick, "The Singing Miner," — Survivor of the 1958 Bump
(Interviewed in 2001)

Author's Note: The Ruddick family served as the inspiration for the story of "Isaak" as written into the novel and screenplay, *Song of Springhill*. Maurice became known as the "Singing Miner" by singing hymns underground to help keep people's spirits up.

1. Tell us about your family life with your husband, Maurice:

He was a good-natured man and loved to joke around. We had a wonderful life there in Springhill. He was very much a family man. When the day the Bump hit, we had twelve children. Our twelfth was only eight days old. Once he was rescued, we were able to have our thirteenth child.

He was a hard worker. He would work double shifts if people couldn't come into work. Sometimes, the whistle would blow to tell them not to come to work, but Maurice would go down anyway, just to make sure.

He loved to load up the kids and take them out for ice cream. They sang together. Anne Murray was always a good friend to our family and the kids. She sang with them and would come over for hours.

Maurice and his buddies would make up songs going down on the rake. They'd sing everything.

2. Did you worry about your husband in this job?

Being the wife of a miner was an accepted way of life. It was the only work. I didn't worry about him until the whistle would blow to signal there was a problem at the mines. I was able to remain a happy-go-lucky person.

3. What happened the night of the Bump and after, while you were waiting for news about him?

When the Bump hit, *I Love Lucy* was on. It sounded similar to thunder, a loud blast but fifteen times louder. I originally thought it was an antenna. Then I saw people running to the mines. A friend came by and gave me the news of the Bump happening. I was so downhearted, waiting for news.

Then a show came on called *Don Messer's Jubilee*, with Charlie Chamberlain. They always ended the show with a hymn, *Farther Along*. I heard the lyrics, "*Farther along, you'll know all about it. Farther along, you'll understand why.*" These words told me that I would have to wait a while before Maurice would come out, but that he would be okay. This gave me the faith.

As time went on, I couldn't listen to any quartets on screen because they reminded me of him. I'd turn off the TV.

My uncle came over, telling me that it was true what the mine officials said, that no one would be left alive. Yet I kept my faith and never gave up hope. I knew he'd be home. After all, God wouldn't leave me with twelve kids to raise alone. Everyone told me not to get my hopes up. Some visited me, like nurses at the hospital. Others brought us food.

My kids would go to mines for hot chocolate while awaiting news. One fellow brought me coal while Maurice was stuck below. I thought it was a gift, but as soon as Maurice was found alive, the same man came back to collect money.

Four or five of my kids had caught the chicken pox, but there was no room at the hospital for them. The hospitals had been cleared for the miners. The kids had to stay at a doctor's house.

4. Did Maurice feel like the No. 2 was a dangerous place to work before the Bump?

Yes, Maurice felt like No. 2 was dangerous and even made up a song about it before the Bump. He called it: *Curse of the Old No. 2*. It was about dangers and taking a chance with their lives. There had been a lot of accidents in that mine. He always believed there would be a big one. There had been a disaster in the No. 1 in 1891 that claimed 125 lives.

5. What did he tell you about his experience once he was rescued?

Once out, Maurice didn't talk about it much. He mentioned rats were crawling near them. Underneath, they sang and prayed, but it was tough with no water. Their throats were so dry. They sang the *Old Rugged Cross*.

Maurice went in with a man who said he was going down to a lower level. Maurice said to go ahead, saying he had stuff to clean up on the level they were at. That guy who went lower died.

They celebrated Garnie's birthday underneath, dividing a chocolate bar into seven pieces. Barney Martin was in a hole alone. They couldn't get him out. They had to crawl on their hands and knees to get stuff to him.

Once Maurice was rescued (as they broke through wall), one of the mine employees said to Maurice that the mine company told this man to find Maurice because he had too many kids to take care of!

I told Maurice he couldn't go back into mines, or I'd leave with our 12 kids. Of course I had nowhere to go.

Maurice wasn't hurt. He just had scratches. Some reported that he had a broken leg, but he didn't. He was in the hospital for one week. But he was like a kid once he got home, and he'd sleep like a baby. I thought he'd have nightmares.

One woman told me, "If it wasn't for Maurice Ruddick, our men would be all dead."

In Loving Memory
Norma June Ruddick
(August 19, 1925 – September 17, 2012)

Norma Ruddick, Cheryl (2001)

Norma & Maurice Ruddick (courtesy of Val Ruddick
MacDonald, photo from inside her CD "Yours Truly")

Cheryl, Valerie (Ruddick) MacDonald (2001)

Valerie Ruddick MacDonald
Daughter of Maurice Ruddick — Survivor of the 1958 Bump
(Interviewed in 2001 and 2014)

1. Your dad became known as "The Singing Miner" because he helped keep people's spirits up underground by singing hymns. He even got an award for his heroic behavior, and his story has inspired many. Tell us about your dad:

Dad was given credit for keeping the miners' morale up during their 8.5 days underground with songs and prayers. He was the recipient of "Canada's Citizen of the Year" Award in 1959 — the only black man to receive such an award. It was supposed to go Prime Minister Diefenbaker at the time. Dad was the eldest miner in his group, 46 years old, and he said the other miners asked him to be responsible for sharing the remaining water and little rations they had left, like chocolate bars and whatever else they had. They must have had great trust in him to do this. Dad always said that they were all heroes, and he was accepting that award for everyone, the rest of the miners and the Town of Springhill.

My dad was a very humble man. He used to say, "I am not a hero."

2. What did your dad like about being a miner?

Dad liked being a miner because he enjoyed the physical labor and camaraderie he shared with the other miners, singing their favorite tunes, sharing jokes as they went down deep into the mines to work. He said they were all equal where the light didn't shine and show the color of a man's skin. His father, Ernest Ruddick, was also a miner before him. At that time, that was the main industry, and it provided a living for the family.

Dad liked to hang out with the other miners after their work week at the Miner's Hall at the top of Main Street where they would play cards, crib, and catch up on the town's news. The Miner's Hall is still there. I believe it is a library now.

3. Tell us what it was like during the Bump:

During the Bump, I was 10 years old. It was a sad time, wondering where our father was. We always watched him come home and go to work at the mines, but women or children never went to the mines. We used to make his lunch for him — honey sandwiches on whole wheat bread, hot tea and honey in his thermos and maybe a piece of cake or cookie.

I would go with my three other sisters every day to the mines and hangout at the Red Cross or Salvation Army tents with others that were waiting to hear news of their loved ones. We were hoping we could bring good news back to Mum. It seemed like there was a deep sadness around the town with so many families looking sad and worried. On the other hand, we didn't have school or household chores to do. There were so many relatives around, people coming and going, media reps for newspapers or magazines, so it was a mixed emotional experience at ten years old. There were boxes of food and clothing available, and it was the first time we had ever tasted Cheese Whiz!

When he came out, he told the rescuers, "Give me water, I'll sing you a song."

4. What happened after the disaster? Did your dad tell you much about it or talk about what it was like underground?
Dad talked very little about what happened underground, the private stuff that miners

protected their families from and what the conditions were really like. Miners went to work, got their pay, and it seemed like everything else was taken care of. I interviewed Dad once for Fundy Cable TV in New Brunswick. He seemed vague about when they had no food and the things they had to do to survive. They had to drink their own urine, for example. Dad, and miners in general, were very private people.

Percy Rector was the one who got his arm caught in a pack. His widow became a good friend of Mom and Dad's. My dad helped him during the Bump by giving him aspirin underground.

When the miraculously rescued miners were invited to Georgia — all 19 of them and their spouses and families — they told us our family would be segregated. Dad's buddies said they didn't want to go if he couldn't stay in the same place. If he was good enough to be underground with them, they should stick together! But my dad suggested they all go anyway and accept the invitation. This was everyone's only chance at this kind of paid vacation. We came from a poor town. No one had any money. So this was a good opportunity. We all dealt with prejudice back then.

I know it wasn't always easy for him. He didn't have to go to Georgia to find racism; it was right at home. Dad taught us to value ourselves and to keep going no matter what.

5. What did your dad do for work after he was done mining?

He was a good father who always provided for his family after the economic hardships of having the mines close after the Bump. Dad cleaned out houses for a living and any odd job he could get. He picked his own coal and wood to store for winter months ahead. He worked at the carpet factory in Springhill as a Commissionaire.

There was a time in the seventies he visited friends in Ontario, who moved there after the mines closed to seek work. He had just won $800 doing the crossword puzzle in the *Halifax Chronicle-Herald* newspaper. He was so excited. During his trip, he stayed with us (me and my husband Barry) when we were living in St. Catharines, Ontario. You would have thought he'd won a million dollars when he and Mum got off the train to meet us. I guess back then, it probably seemed like it. He brought an extra suitcase of goodies he purchased with some of the winnings, like coffee, tea bags, crabmeat and sardines. Everywhere he went, somebody got a treat. He also gave each of us thirteen kids $10.

6. Talk about how you and your dad and your siblings used to sing together.

He would whistle and sing around the house. He also had a whistling tune he used to call the hens and roosters from the hen house to come for their scratch and feed (made from some concoction he made of left over burnt bread or veggie peelings). Those hens would come running like crazy because they knew his tune. Then he taught it to us. Other times he'd gather us up on a Saturday night and put on a concert in the yard for our neighbors. We'd all be singing and laughing.

Dad always sang and played a 4-string guitar that he improved, and it sounded as good as a fancier one. It was his trademark. He loved to play a reel-to-reel tape recorder and taped most of the early days when he would teach us to sing and practice harmonies. This would have been in the early sixties.

After the Bump, he trained me and two of my sisters, Sylvia and Ellen, to sing harmonies. He would often sing the bass voice and lead. We all took turns learning. When he felt we were ready, he'd spread the news and soon we'd do a lot of performing with him throughout Nova Scotia and New Brunswick. We were known as "Maurice Ruddick the Singing Miner and the Minerettes." We would practice in a side room off the kitchen and Mum would be mending our clothes. It would seem like long hours, especially when we wanted to go to school dances.

Today, we are so grateful for all that Dad taught us of our musical abilities. Because of what he taught us, we were able to sing a variety of songs; harmonies just came naturally to us. We sang Beatles tunes and Mum would style our hair like theirs in those days. Mum used Vaseline to pat our curly hair down.

We sang tunes by Johnny Cash, Bobby Vinton, Irish music, Negro spirituals, hymns, barbershop, jazz, whatever was on the hit parade. He would tackle it all and us girls with him. He even taught us to make musical sounds like a horn with our mouths; he could imitate the sound of a horn like it was real!

Dad started another group with my siblings that consisted of Leah, Iris, Trina, Jesse and Maureen. They were called "The Harmony Babes." They performed throughout Nova Scotia and New Brunswick as well.

It truly was the Spirit that kept his passion for music going. Spiritually, he'd say, "Talk to the man upstairs," meaning our Lord.

7. Tell us more about your father's history:

He was born in Joggins, Nova Scotia, and lived there as a young boy until his Mum died when he was 9. His father worked in Springhill after that. In Dad's time, you only needed a Grade 11 education to be a high school grad; he was proud that he achieved this level. After the mines closed, he attended Vocational School to get his Grade 12.

Dad's kindness was felt throughout our community. For instance, when he went fishing and hunting to provide for our family, he always shared with our neighbors, especially the elders who were bedridden due to illness. When the Salvation Army would get deer meat donated to share in our community, they gave it to Dad to divide and share. They knew he could be trusted to ensure that everyone had some.

At Christmas, the Red Cross and Salvation Army and the Lions Club brought out a turkey and candy and vegetables for us, which made our Christmas for the family.

Sometimes, we would come home from school for lunch at noon and Mum would have a large pot on the stove full of skim milk and peas with bread and molasses—a staple diet—and a dipper full of tea and sugar but mostly milk. Dad always made sure we had something to eat. We never went hungry, and Mum kept the homemade bread plentiful, up to ten loaves a day.

Dad started to suffer from severe arthritis; it eventually crippled him. He was confined to a wheelchair. My dad died when he was 75 years old, in 1988.

He was a good husband to our mother, a good father, and a man of inspiration to the rest of us, and many others who know his story.

* * *

Valerie shared the lyrics from two songs her father wrote about the mines:

Curse of the Old No. 2
Lyrics by Maurice Ruddick
You've heard of Springhill's big producer,
her history's of crimson hue.
But the biggest tale the old miners tell,
is the curse on old number two.

Brought miners from all over the country,
the drillers and all their crew.
A drilling to find the curse and the bumps,
that haunted old number two.

Away Down in the Deeps
Lyrics by Maurice Ruddick
Turn out your lights, boys,
and I will sing you a song.
I will give you a heartache,
as trolleys roll along.

I will sing you a song, boys,
away down here in the deeps.
Where the miners go to make their dough,
and there isn't much time for sleep.

Away down in the deeps, boys,
it is a peaceful life.
A place we know where we can go,
to get clear of a nagging wife.

If we should die in the deeps, boys,
we know where we will go,
Heaven, boys, is away way above,
and hell is right here below.

Author's Note: Val assures me that her mother thought the lyrics to this second song were quite funny, even with the nagging wife comment.

To inquire about Val's original music, contact:
macsigns@rogers.com

Rescuers &
Family of
Rescuers

Bill Booth
Son of Jim Booth, who worked as a barefaced rescuer during both mine disasters
(Interviewed in 2001 and 2013)

1. Where were you when the 1958 Bump happened and what did you do?

When the Bump occurred, I was sitting in the living room in a large chair watching TV. Then I was on the floor, and the house was shaking. My father, Jim, came running down the stairs and he said, "Something happened at the mines." Then he left for the pit head. We didn't see him until 48 hours later.

2. What was your father's role in the rescue operations? And why was he involved?

My father was one of the barefaced draegermen to first go into the mines. They didn't have gas masks on. They crawled on their hands and knees, looking for survivors. He wanted to do whatever he could to help.

When he'd come home, he was stressed out and said it was bad but didn't talk about it very much. He'd rest and then go right back out, and the worrying would start all over again. All you could do was hope for the best. My dad never complained about the danger.

3. What did you do during the rescues?

I would go the pit head and wait for news, but I wouldn't see my father for a long time. I usually waited with another kid waiting for his father who was in the Bump. He wouldn't know if his dad were alive, while I was wondering if my dad, as a rescuer, was going to make it out alive. There was talk about the methane gas below.

Some of the Army Cadets (like your dad) were involved in directing traffic and others were sent to the pit head to help form a human fence to keep the people back. They needed help. So some of the older Boy Scouts, like me, filled in for them when they needed a rest. We weren't old enough to drive and yet we were directing traffic.

4. What was Springhill like after the final rescues?

That Christmas was a very sad one for the town of Springhill, especially those who had loved ones lost in the Bump. But it affected everyone because they were neighbors, classmates, people you grew up with. Sometimes, you'd see a kid get a bike for Christmas, but the ones who lost their dads wouldn't because their mothers couldn't afford it.

5. Share about how your father was honored for his bravery during these rescue operations:

There were four other men who were draegermen that were involved with The Boy Scouts of Canada. My dad was a Scout Master in the Anglican Church for the Boy Scouts of Canada. These five men were awarded the "Silver Cross" for bravery. The "Silver Cross" was presented to them by the Governor General of Canada in the Parliament Buildings in Ottawa, Ontario. All five men stated that all of the barefaced draegermen where just as brave as them, but because they were not involved in the Boy Scouts, they were not recognized.

**Ken Warren
Retired Mining Engineer,
Worked in Springhill mines prior to the
1956 disaster, Rescuer
(Interviewed in 2001)**

1. What did you do for the mines when you worked there?
In 1953-56, I worked underground for the department of mines and natural resources. I decided to do a thesis on the rocks.

2. There's a lot of controversy about the cause of the Bump. What can you share about this?
There's a theory that the Bump was caused by strong measures in No. 2 seam. The ground below No. 2's seam was at strong risk of bump occurrence. Bumps had occurred there.

My theory about the cause of the Bump is this: the rocks below the seam were layered with coal, then soft, then hard sandstone. When the stress built up, the softer stuff would blow out. They had aligned the walls. The strong layer broke due to stress.

Before they started lining up the walls (using the long wall system), they had used the step system, mining with pillar and room method. Pillars held up the roof. Then they started to have trouble with pillars bursting or deteriorating. Many were killed in the twenties due to this.

A German engineer said mining wouldn't be possible below 4000 feet because coal was too weak any lower to withstand pressure at that vertical depth. So the engineer recommended for Springhill's No. 2 to change to the long wall system and not do room and pillar. The walls in long wall were 400 feet long each, its levels 13,000, 13,400, and 13,800. But in a step system, they are offset by 100 feet or 50 feet. This change made it a 400-foot break first, then the next one, then the next one.

3. Do you think this long wall method caused the Bump?

It was the theory of the miners that had worked there. They felt the walls should never have been lined up because then it would be too long at 1200 ft. And that is what happened. But was it the cause of this deadly disaster? It's hard to tell.

4. What did you do during the rescue operation?

I was not a draegerman. I went down as a barefaced miner during the rescue. It actually wasn't legal because I was no longer an employee. But they forgot and let me help. I had done some odd jobs to help, carrying water bottles for the draeger crew when they'd come back to the fresh air base in between work.

Dr. Arnold Burden
Former Miner,
Doctor / Rescuer during both disasters
(Interviewed in 2001)

What a privilege it was for my father and I to sit down with Dr. Arnold Burden and hear of his adventures. Not only had he worked as a miner, he was involved as a doctor in both rescue missions for the 1956 Explosion and the 1958 Bump. His Army training also prepared him for helping victims or dealing with casualties.

Dr. Burden was a physician in Springhill and on Prince Edward Island. When he worked as a miner, he was still in school studying to become a doctor. He worked in the No. 1 and No. 4 during summers. The other miners were always careful with him, making sure he didn't injure himself or his hands. They'd tell him to put gloves on or to stay between the packs and not come near the coal face because of the bumps. They'd have bumps practically every day. They actually liked those small ones because it loosened the coal. They didn't have to dig or pick, just shovel it into the pan, and go home early.

The whole wall got paid based on production, as a team. Burden described a typical mining shift. "We'd cut the coal, pull it out, put it in the packs, and then move the pans. We had to deal with the gob (waste), too. Once it was time to pull the packs, we'd let it collapse."

When the 1956 Explosion happened, Burden was on Prince Edward Island. There was no ferry for him to take over that night so he had to wait until morning. "I packed about $800 worth of drugs and dressings and went to Springhill. I knew the hospital there. I stayed at my wife's family home. I helped some of the burn cases. In one case, I had to ask who the person was in order to officially pronounce him dead. It turned out he was someone I had gone to school with." The first victim's name he heard was Pleaman Pyke, who Burden had grown up near.

Burden said, "They were asking for a doctor at the pit head the morning after the Explosion. No one had come out alive yet except for a couple at the surface. So I packed equipment in my pocket. There was not much to do at the hospital since people hadn't been found alive yet. I went to the mines, got dressed up, and went underground. Two draegermen were killed 200 feet from the surface. Some at the surface saw them go down.

"I had worked in that mine in the auxiliary

slope (rescue tunnel). One day, the hoist broke, and I had to walk up through the rescue tunnel. It was a sixty-degree angle. Rescuers were collapsing in the tunnel. So I started crawling on my hands and knees to rescue the rescuers and draegermen. I used one of their tanks and used my hands as a tunnel over their noses. I also collapsed once myself in a tunnel, on top of those I was supposed to rescue. It's like they'd send three men down to go get one, then all four would collapse down there because of gas. Eventually, we'd get them up. I had one on my back, then a second one, both unconscious. While helping these two, I passed out. I landed in a hole where I could breathe again."

Dr. Burden had to recover at a fresh air base, an area that didn't have gas. They blew the fans to keep it clear.

Dr. Burden described what caused the disaster: "Three explosions had occurred. Thirteen boxcars came up the slope with coal in them. Twelve boxcars let go and rolled back down. They hit a steep and rolled off and hit a high-tension line. It blew coal, which caused the Explosion.

"I went back down the next day, too. Saturday. It helped that I knew the shaft."

During the rescue efforts after the Explosion, when they started to believe no one who wasn't already above ground had survived, the rescuers realized there was a large group of men alive. Fifty of them! (**Author's Note**: this includes Ken Melanson, who was interviewed for this book.)

"Once they broke through to where the men were, I went down to them. I had to contend with fifty people on my own. The other doctor they sent down got stuck with another guy. Six men of the fifty needed stretchers to get out. I would treat people and then send them up.

"I had a bottle of rum with me. Bob Smith, one of the men who'd been stuck underground, said it was the best rum he'd ever had in his life.

"Some men were face down, unconscious. I thought they were dead. But actually, some were alive. By the point when we found the fifty, the gas was cleared, but there was no oxygen. It took six men to move a stretcher. It was tough to breathe down there.

"To get up the slope, the draeger team had put in a haulage thing. They rigged one with a pulley. I wanted the men who needed a stretcher up first. I sent rescuers with a guy on a stretcher so that rescuer could hold onto the man and keep them from falling and killing those below."

In a tense moment, an engineer showed him a note. It said: *Evacuate the mine with all possible haste.*

Burden said, "They put a tube through to take air samples. This stuff explodes at 20%. The reading came to 19%. If that had exploded, there were so many doctors up and down the slope. Fifty-two men below it, and the hundreds of people on surface. If it had blown, it could have killed 500 or more people. All the trapped miners, plus all the rescuers could have died, easily. It was so close to exploding again. That's why they said hurry up and evacuate right now."

Yet, when this warning came, Burden still had forty people to contend with. Plus there were two men further down. These men had gone without food and water for five days. He finally got the men moved up except the two. He needed two more stretchers for them. He and Buddy Condy were there with the two men. They wondered if those above forgot them, but when Burden went to check, people were still working.

Once he was sure the rest were dead and there was no one else to rescue, Burden went back to his practice on Prince Edward Island. Yet he was always ready to return whenever Springhill ran into trouble, like during the 1957 Fire and the 1958 Bump.

When the Bump happened, he actually felt the rattle in his building. "It felt like a low flying plane dropped three bombs."

When he got to the mines, they gave him coveralls and a lamp. They had heard it was pretty bad down there. He and three others went down after 9 p.m., most of which had no gas masks on. They went down the back slope, helping some men along the way. They weren't terribly hurt, like walking wounded. (**Author's Note**: my grandfather was likely one of those men he crossed paths with on the way down.)

Their safety lamps kept going out, and they couldn't relight. The gas wasn't too bad; they kept on going down and got beyond the gas.

"We got to Leon Melanson. Only part of his face and shoulder could be seen. The rest was under coal. I gave him a shot of Demerol and kept going down. Four hours later, I knew it would wear off, so I went back to help him. I saw a foot under his armpit. The other guys thought there was a dead man under him and that foot belonged to the other guy. They wanted to take the leg off the dead man. But I suspected that wasn't another person's foot. I told them to keep on digging. There actually was someone else under him, but the foot belonged to Leon himself. It had broken off. He did lose his leg once he was in the hospital.

"As I went to other levels, like the 13,400, I couldn't recognize them because they were so damaged. We couldn't get near 13,000.

"Two men were trapped where draegermen couldn't get to because of the packs on their backs. They tried to get over and couldn't. After he'd been underground for fourteen hours, they had to send another lamp down.

"One new rescuer had a chocolate bar in his pocket. So I asked him, 'When did you eat last?' The guy said he'd eaten a little while ago. So I asked him if I could have it since I hadn't had a bite to eat."

As bodies were taken out, each one had to be identified by the doctor, a mine official, and a union official. They all had to sign how the identification was made and how they died. They used tags to identify the body and put another tag on the casket. Caskets were sealed because of the smell. It was over 70 degrees down there. They'd call the minister of a fallen miner and have that minister go break the official news to the family. They tried to arrange for that to happen first, so the name wouldn't be released to the press until the family knew.

"I filled out a book of death certificates as they identified them and gave them check numbers. I kept a list of what they died of. But then I got a call that men were found alive. A mine worker heard men talking through the pipes. I was in the mine manager's office when names of the twelve were called. When I heard they wanted to put Vitamin B in the water they were sending through the pipes, I overruled them. I knew if they did that, the men would throw it back up.

"So I went back down and got them water. We tried to feed them first through a plastic hose, but it bent. Then I asked for 100 feet of copper tubing and pushed it through. Gorley Kempt asked for more water. So, we sent more. Gorley yelled that he didn't have anything to put the water in and was afraid they were wasting it. But we assured him: there was more water available. We had to pressurize it with a tree sprayer to get it to go downward, since it was more like straight across. The wall between us and the miners was parallel.

"It took eighty-two feet of digging to get to those men. It was all virgin coal, never been cut before. It wasn't just debris we had to break through to get to the twelve trapped men. The men had no idea how far away we were. We just kept saying, 'We're coming. Rest. Take it easy.' We didn't want to tell them how far we were. It took fourteen hours to cut that tunnel. It was a very small space for all these people. We couldn't stand. Any debris had to be removed in an assembly line. Everyone sitting in the tunnel had to pass back buckets. We used sawed off picks and shovels. Whoever was in front had the hardest job, so we'd take turns.

"The rescue group got longer throughout the tunnel, as it was a longer way to pass back coal. Once we broke through, it filled with coal dust. Ten were in one place and two were off in another area. One had a bone out through his skin. The other had a broken shoulder. The ten had been able to bring water to the other two. They just couldn't move the men up to the rest of the group because of a lack of tools and equipment. They shared everything they had left and used an aspirin bottle cap to divide up water, before the rescue." (**Author's Note**: Caleb Rushton, who was interviewed for this book, was one of the men in this first big group of twelve rescued.)

After the first miracle rescue of the twelve, Burden got word that more men were alive underground, that Springhill was experiencing another miraculous rescue. By this point, it had been eight days since the Bump.

"We got Barney Martin out through the hole first; he had been stuck alone, away from the other six. We got a stretcher for him and shipped him out. Then two others had started up. It was a domed ceiling with no support. The rescuers made it to the last six people. They got right to these guys. We didn't need to send them any food.

"Maurice Ruddick said, 'My God, I'm glad to see you fellas. Give me a glass of water, I'll sing you a song.' Then Bobby Calder said, 'Maurice, I was sent down specifically to get you out.' Maurice asked, 'What do you mean?' Bobby joked, 'The compensation board told me with your wife and twelve kids, there'd be no money for anybody else.'" (**Author's Note**: Herb Pepperdine, also interviewed for this book, was with Maurice's group during this final rescue.)

Eighty-one men were rescued the first night. (One of those would die later in the hospital.) Taking into account the two miracle rescues of twelve and seven men, of the 174 men trapped underground, 99 of them lived and 75 of them died. No doubt it's due to the rescue efforts of Dr. Burden and many others that they were able to save as many people as they did.

Dr. Arnold Burden, Cheryl (2001)

Children of

Victims

Jerry Gillis
Son of Angus Gillis — Victim of the 1958 Bump
(Interviewed in 2001)

Angus "Gus" Gillis was one of the miracle survivors of the 1956 Explosion; he was stuck with a group of 50 men underground, long after they thought everyone was dead. The men waited with their leader, Con Embree, and were eventually rescued. However, when the 1958 Bump hit, Gus was not one of the survivors.

Jerry Gillis, son of Gus Gillis, was in the military at the time of the Bump. He had made arrangements to come home when he first heard about it. However, by the time he got there, his father was already declared dead, a victim of the poisonous gasses that filled the mines after the Bump. They knew cause of death because there were no signs of injury when they found him.

Jerry recalls how many in town felt like the way they mined the coal caused the Bump to happen, by trying to line up the walls. However, he believes if people like his father were worried about their safety, they mostly just kept it to themselves. They talked to other miners about it instead of concerning their families.

Like to other kids in the area, mining was considered a way of life. "I never worried about my dad," said Gillis in an interview in 2001. "I was much more into kid stuff before the disasters. People getting hurt just seemed to be a fact of life in Springhill. It seemed like during my teen years, someone was always getting killed. It was an accepted part of life." His mother even seemed to be calm, to not worry about his father's safety underground. If she was concerned, she hid it well. His grandfathers were also miners, so it ran in the family. It was definitely not an easy life.

When Jerry turned 16, there were only a couple of work options for those in Springhill: drive a truck or work in the mines. He never considered following in his father's or grandfathers' footsteps. He joined the Army instead, at 16, with his parents' permission, so he could join a special program. He did this so he wouldn't have to work in the mines.

One of Jerry's memories of Springhill is that when it would snow, it would be a very pretty white for a couple of days. Not long after that fresh blanket of white fell, it would turn dark from the coal dust floating in the air.

He remembers fondly that the town was "very close knit, where everyone knew each other."

Jerry Gillis, Cheryl (2001)

Jack & Keith Bourgeois
Former Miners,
Sons of Bliss Bourgeois — Victim of the 1958 Bump
Nephews of Herb Pepperdine
(Interviewed in 2001)

Even though Jack and Keith were also rescuers, I decided to put them in this section of the book to honor their father with the other children of lost miners. When I did the interview with Bump survivor, Herb Pepperdine, his nephews were with him. I had the opportunity to sit down with Jack and Keith, two brothers who lost their father in the Bump. Sadly, Keith has since passed away. Jack and Keith were very helpful to me, in supplying research about some of the ins and outs of working in a mine and how the place operated, what the workers did underground if they were a miner vs. a laborer. They were enormously helpful in explaining those differences, and all of that was used when developing the jobs for characters in my screenplay and novel, *Song of Springhill.*

They described the process laborers went through. They'd build the packs that helped the roof not cave in on the miners. They'd also put coal in pans. Jack said, "The pans looked like a coffee table, but they were steel. Miners took coal off the wall from the coal face in front of them, and put them into the pans. They used two big machines, on the end and top of the wall. The coal would shake down into the level, and then we'd fill coal cars. Someone like Herb, a laborer, would take a trip up once it was full. Then he'd come back with the empties. As the coal face got further away from pans, there was a higher chance that the roof would cave in, so they'd put packs in to hold the roof up behind you. The laborers built those packs. As the wall got further from pans, the overnight shift at 11 p.m. had the job of moving those pans closer to the wall."

This was one of the jobs that Jack had when he worked the overnight shift. "We'd drag the pans for the miners starting the next day. We'd have to reuse the same pack, take a handsaw to it, cut the pack then take a wedge. A short block. We'd knock the block out in a couple of places then the pack could be reused. You'd hope it wouldn't collapse on you while you were doing it!"

When I first started to research this story, I had a hard time understanding the differences between how they mined in the No. 4—which some felt was less dangerous than the system they adopted in the No. 2. (The old system was room and pillar; the new system was long wall.) Jack described how this worked: "In the old system, a slope would be diagonal. In the new system, walls lined up so at the top you'd look down like you're looking through a straight tunnel. Think of how this would affect something like a bowling ball. If staggered — like in the No. 4 — the bowling ball would have stopped at one of the levels. Instead, it went all the way down to the bottom. It had a ripple effect."

We talked about what it was like for them the day of the Explosion. Jack had gone hunting and missed the Explosion. Keith had just gotten home at 4 p.m. Both of them got involved in the rescue efforts.

Keith mentioned that those he went down with in the rescue efforts would get overcome by gas. They'd have to be brought out of the mines on stretchers. "When we were at the 4400 level, we didn't dare lift our head more than five to six inches off the ground, crawling, or we'd get taken over by afterdamp, the gasses in the air."

After Con Embree's group was found, Jack was one of the first two miners to reach the men, at the 5400 level. "Doug Beaton was lying in a stone dust box. We thought he was dead, but he wasn't. He was covered with empty stone dust bags and his nostrils were full of dust. After we got the 5400 level men out, they sealed the mines until January to get the fire to go out. There was a great fear it would blow up again. There were more miners in the mine doing rescue work than trapped miners."

Keith shared, "Once rescued, most of the miners ended up in the unemployment line. They got physically checked out to make sure they were okay, but no other help."

Jack recalled, "When I worked underground, I worked near my dad but not with him. I used to go down and visit his level on days I didn't have much to do."

Keith recalls having lunch underground with his friend, Alfred White, telling him that there had to be a better way to make a living; Keith quit that day after that conversation. Keith recalls, "On March 18, 1958, there was a small bump, right where we were sitting, eating lunch." Alfred died that day as a result of injuries from that bump. (He was the only one who died, that particular day in the mine.) Keith was thankful he didn't feel there was a future in it; he could have been right there with Alfred.

Jack and Keith had both joined the Air Force before the big Bump in October 1958, so neither was there when that happened. But their father, Bliss, was underground.

Jack heard about the Bump on the news, from

where he was working in the military. He couldn't get through by phone. "I had to come to town to get any news. My mother had already died by this point. I sat around and waited at the Wash House, under his bucket. Our dad was working at the 13,800 level.

"During the Bump, we had overheard other miners talking about how bad it was underground. They'd said no one else survived. Then, I heard a rumor that my father was with the group of twelve who were being rescued when those names were called. However, I didn't quite believe it and never rejoiced in it. Then my dad wasn't with those men. It took about a week before we officially heard confirmation that he was dead."

On a lighter note, the two shared some fun antics that happened among the miners when they worked there. It gave me some fun material for the scenes in the screenplay and novel underground.

"If a miner fell a sleep, like at lunch, other miners would tie their shoes together so he'd trip when he got up. Or they'd nail his lunch can on the pack by the bottom, so when he'd go to pick up the lunch pail, his arm would stretch two feet because the lunch pail wouldn't go anywhere.

"We always had to tease the newcomers. They'd be told by older miners to get a shovel with the name Jones on it. The newbie would go down below to get one and another miner would say, 'Where are you going with my shovel?' The newbie would say, 'It belongs to a miner up there named Jones.' And they'd be embarrassed to find out all shovels say Jones because it's the manufacturer.

"Another interesting thing we had to do was tie our pants with boot laces to keep rats from crawling up our pant legs. It was terrible if it went up. You'd have to jump around and shake to get it out."

I also asked them what they did for fun in Springhill, so I'd have some material for the kids in my fictional story. "We loved to hop cars. We'd hang onto cars without drivers seeing us, and it was like we were skating or skiing down a hill by hanging onto the back of the bumper. We'd do this when it had snowed. Our mittens would stay stuck on the bumper once we let go, and of course, we'd get in trouble going home with one mitten. We'd also play a game racing tires. We'd use a steel rim and an old rubber tire and chase it all around town. We'd use the stick to make the tire roll, then steer it."

They also shared they'd go see movies about three days a week, the Saturday matinee, Wednesday matinee, and Friday night, 7 p.m. show. It was fifteen cents to get in. The town also had musical or variety shows since there was a lot of musical talent in town.

"Saturday was payday. The miners would come into town, go shopping, and go talk mining on their days off on Main Street. Downtown was busy on Saturday night. Live, old time bands would play during skating. We could skate all night Friday, all day Saturday and Sunday."

I so enjoyed interviewing these guys to get such a variety of perspectives that helped me build scenes for the fictional story.

In Loving Memory
Keith Ronald Bourgeois
(April 14, 1935-February 7, 2012)

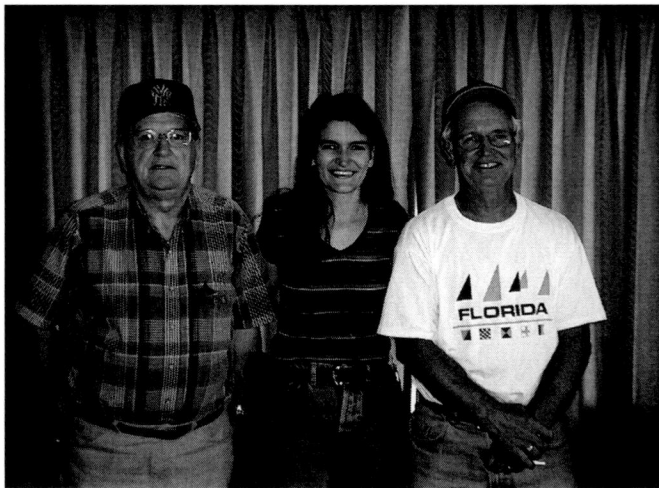

Keith, Cheryl, Jack (2001)

Valarie Tabor Alderson
Daughter of Raymond "Tommy" Tabor — Victim
of the 1958 Bump
(Interviewed in 2014)

Author's Note: I would like to personally thank Valarie for the many favors she did for me over the decade of working on this book and *Song of Springhill*.

1. What can you tell me about Springhill in the fifties?

I can remember living on lower Herrett Road when I was a kid. We lived on one side of a double house and my father's parents lived on the other end. It was just up the road from the mine. The house below us had a store in their living room where they sold penny candy. My grandmother would give us a few pennies for doing errands for her and of course, it was all spent on candy! I can remember a little "shack" in the backyard where my grandfather and his friends would gather to play checkers and cards (most likely had the occasional nip). My grandmother was a Baptist who frowned upon playing cards, but she loved to go to Bingo. After my grandfather no longer worked in the mines, he would wait for his sons to stop in and tell him about their day in the pit.

I remember when I was in Grade 1, we moved up to the opposite end of town to help my mother's parents, as they were getting elderly and needed the assistance. My mother's father was a miner and also an avid gardener. He grew a lot of his own vegetables and would spend hours in his garden after his shift in the mine. However, he was retired from mining by the time we moved in with them.

During those years, we all played outside all day long and into the evening. We always walked to school, played ball, tag, etc. with our friends. People would often gather and sing songs in each other's houses. I remember neighbors visiting each other and spending lots of time chatting.

You never missed mass on Sundays and the first Friday each month we had to attend morning mass. We had to go to Sunday School every week and you had to know the answers from the catechism. At Christmas time, you were allowed to take one toy and then we were off to visit family and friends. We made sure we visited all the relatives during the holidays.

I have some fond memories of the vacations in the summer. The mines would shut down for two weeks when everyone went on vacation. My dad always made sure we went somewhere on a little trip. I have a photo of my younger sister, Susan, and I with my dad taken on the PEI ferry the summer of 1958. That was our last family vacation.

I always liked school and was a good student with pretty good marks. I went to university after Grade 11.

My older sister was a teenager, and she and her friends would spend time at "The Stand." It reminded me of Happy Days, where they hung out, talked, and listened to the jukebox. They, too, ate hamburgers, drank milkshakes and had lots of fun with their friends.

The town was bustling then with stores lined up and down Main Street. We had clothing shops, a shoe shop, jewelry stores, a theatre, bakery etc. I guess it was like most other small towns in Nova Scotia. It is so sad to see it today with the modern buildings and empty lots. The majority of the original buildings are gone. It was a one-industry town and never recovered economically after the 1958 Bump.

2. Do you remember anything about the 1956 Explosion? Where were you when it happened? Was your father working?

I remember playing outside about 5 p.m. with my friends on the street. We heard a loud noise and looked up and saw a huge, black mushroom cloud. At first we didn't know what it was. My father was at home, and he quickly jumped into his car and went toward the mine. My grandparents lived on lower Herrett Road, which was very close to the mine. I don't know why, but my brother, my cousin and I ran from our house, way up on Pleasant Street, all the way out to my grandparents' home. I remember people milling around the yard and talking about what happened. Everyone was outside and looking down toward the mine. They talked about an explosion.

It turned out that two of my uncles were working that day. One was rescued and later moved to the Boston area. My Uncle Donald died from gas. He was only 34. It was a very sad day.

I still can't believe that we ran all that way out there; I was only 7 years old. It would be over a mile at least. My uncle who moved away to Boston tried to convince my father to go, but he wouldn't leave Springhill.

3. What were the men like who worked with your father? Were they friends outside of work?

My dad was only 38 years old when he was killed. (He had two other brothers who were killed in the mines. One died in a single rock fall, and the other in the Explosion.) He was a little league baseball coach. He was also a member of the Knights of Columbus and had all the decorations at our house for their annual Harvest Ball. Growing up, many of the guys he had coached would often speak about how much they liked him.

I think most of the men who worked in the mines got along. They were always joking around. I think they worked hard and drank too much. When we lived out in the west end of town, the men gathered around the Liars Bench and would often stay up late into the night talking. It was told to me that my grandfather, Percy Tabor, was the President of the Liars Bench and could tell some great stories.

I will relate one that was told to me. One summer day, a tourist stopped at the Liars Bench and asked to speak to the President of the Liars Club. Apparently, the tourist was a well-known teller of tall tales from the town where he lived in the U.S.A. He challenged my grandfather to a lying contest. My grandfather graciously let him go first since he was the visitor. I don't recall his story, but apparently it was quite an outrageous lie. So, he challenged my grandfather to top that one. My grandfather took his time pondering and then said, "I think I can better that one. I believe you!" We had a pretty good laugh about that one.

My grandfather belonged to the Royal Order of Buffaloes. They would often take turns taking lunch for their meetings. My father went to the store up the street and bought some expensive luncheon meat, sliced cooked ham for his sandwiches. He brought the meat home to my aunt and asked her to make the sandwiches for him to take to the lodge meeting. After he left for the meeting, my aunt noticed that the cooked ham was still sitting on the counter in the pantry. She realized she had buttered and put mustard on the bread and forgot to put the meat in between. She and my grandmother agreed they wouldn't say a word to my dad about it. When he came home that night, they asked how the meeting went. His reply was that it was fine, but he said, "Can you imagine some cheap son-of-a-gun brought mustard sandwiches for lunch?" We often have a great chuckle about that.

4. Where were you when the 1958 Bump happened? And how old were you?

The Bump happened shortly after 8 p.m. on a Thursday night. I was in Grade 4 and nine years old. I remember standing by the kitchen table and finishing my homework when I felt the shaking. I had no idea what it was. We lived with my maternal grandparents at the time. My mother was in the kitchen by the stove, and my grandmother came out to the kitchen from the living room. I remember her starting to cry and she said, "My God, it's the mine." She knew immediately what happened, as she had felt many of them before. The next morning, my mother told us about what happened and said we would have to wait and see. My older sister and brother went out to the mine every day to wait for news and report back to our mother. I was not allowed to go out there, as I was only 9. (Although, there were lots of kids who went out there and hung around waiting for news of their fathers.)

5. Share some other details about the Bump and your father's story:

I remember lots of confusion surrounding that night. My father was working the afternoon shift and so were three of my uncles. My mother's brothers. Both families had men who worked in the mine. I remember the phone ringing and people coming in and out of the house, all talking about the disaster.

It turned out that all three of my mother's brothers got out. One of her brothers was knocked unconscious. When he came to, he was buried in coal up to his chest. He often remarked that if he had been thrown down, he would surely have died. It turned out he was thrown back against what they called a pack stick—a piece of timber they used to secure the wall and roof. One other brother walked out and, yet the third brother was a supervisor at the time. He began to assist with the rescue effort.

My mother told us that my father was late for work that day, as he had a meeting at the Company office. She said when he went to pick up his lamp, it wasn't working and he had to borrow one. Apparently, she was told he had to run to catch the "rake" (trolley) to go to work. She found that odd. Any other time, he would have likely just come home and made the time up later, as it was around the time of the World Series.

Until she passed away, she kept his shoes with a cake of ivory soap in them. They were in the Wash House. My sister still has them now.

6. What did you do while waiting for news?

Within the next couple of days, I was sent across the street to stay with neighbors. I guess they offered to take me so it would make it easier on my mother. I had an older sister who was 16 and a brother who was 12 at the time. I was 9. I also had a younger sister who was 4.

I read the newspaper every day and watched TV. The neighbors were an older couple, and they tried to shield me from the talk of the disaster. I can still remember one day when the man who drove the dry cleaning truck was talking with the lady who was looking after me. He expressed how sad it was across the street (my house) because of my father most likely being killed.

I will never forget reading the newspaper and reading the list of missing men. I got so excited one day when I didn't see my father's name on that list. I can still remember the heartache I felt when I noticed "to be continued" at the bottom of the column and his name was there on the next page. I would cry myself to sleep at night and often imagine that he would come home soon.

Another thing I will never forget is my brother and uncle coming over to where I was staying. My brother took me outside to tell me they found our father. He was only 12 but insisted he be the one to tell me. I was naïve and asked him if dad was alive. He just looked at me and said "no." My brother was the altar boy for my father's funeral. I never attended the funeral, as I was so devastated. I was asked if I wanted to be there and I said "no." To this day, I regret that I didn't go.

During those days, the caskets were brought to the homes because the funeral parlour was so small. His funeral was at the same time as another miner who went to our church. There were so many funerals that they had to double up some of them.

My brother passed away when he was only 43 in 1990. It broke my mother's heart. When she was interviewed for an oral history of the town and disasters, she constantly cried.

My father was Protestant and his father and brothers belonged to the Orange Lodge. My mother was a Catholic. When they married, he turned Catholic and his brother refused to attend his funeral. How times have changed.

7. Is there anything else you can think of to tell about that time?

I remember how sad it was for all the kids at the time of the Bump. I remember there were at least three of us in the same Grade 4 class who lost our dads. At Christmas time, we all received many gifts. You could tell the kids who lost their dads, as we all had yellow hooded sweatshirts. The boys all got Toronto Maple Leaf sweaters and autographed hockey sticks from the team. (During the 50th Anniversary, my son arranged to get another stick autographed from the team and gave it to the Miner's Museum to be on display.) I must say that I have never liked Christmas since that time.

We didn't have the benefit of psychologists or counselors. We were left on our own to deal with our grief. Many other kids (such as my husband) felt the survivor's guilt because their fathers weren't killed in the mines. Many of their friends' fathers died. It seemed like there wasn't a person in Springhill who wasn't affected by the tragedy. Everyone had a brother, uncle, dad, or friend that were victims. I can't really blame the adults for not helping the kids because I think they were just trying to manage to bury our dead. It must have been unbelievably stressful for everyone in town.

Families packed up and left and many of the surviving miners had difficulty finding work. Many of the women went out to work. My mother had little education and four children to care for.

The Mayor of Calgary, Alberta, offered to take us out there and start over. However, she felt that she couldn't do that. At least if she stayed in Springhill, she'd have other family members around her. So one of my uncles (my mother's brother) took his family out there instead. He made a living out there and eventually moved to British Columbia where he remained until he died.

One of my proudest accomplishments was when I went to the Town Council and presented them with a plan for the 50th Anniversary. We filled the Community Centre for two evenings with a full house for the Memorial Service and concert featuring the "Men of the Deeps" choir. It was a heart-healing event. Many people came to us — the committee members — afterwards and thanked us for the opportunity to heal some of the wounds. We had national newspaper and TV coverage for the event. I must say it was my son who pushed me to do something. I truly believe I was guided by either the Holy Spirit or something bigger than me. I had no idea what I wanted to do.

As I sat alone one evening, it came to me! I wanted to have a candlelight vigil with 75 people holding a lit candle (each one representing a lost miner from the Bump). As each name was read, the candle was blown out. I didn't want to leave people without hope, so I decided that I would have 19 people on stage with miners' helmets on. They represented those who were found after 6 and 8 days trapped underground. As each rescued miner's name was read, the light was turned on to signify hope. We ended with the song "Rise Again." I wanted everyone to remember how we rose from the tragedy and still survived.

The song says, "We rise again in the faces of our children."

Susan, Raymond "Tommy" Tabor, Valarie (1956)

Ethel Fisher Gilbert
Daughter of Lester Fisher — Victim of the 1956 Explosion
(Interviewed in 2014)

Author's Note: As you know from the stories about my grandfather, he switched shifts with someone the day of the Explosion. It took me a while to research this story and figure out who that person may have been. From Ken Melanson's interview, you heard him give us two potential names, the two men who had the same job as my grandfather: Lester Fisher and Gerald Dawson.

My father felt like my grandfather normally worked with Gerald. That left us leaning toward the idea that he possibly switched with Lester. Then, in my research of newspaper articles, I found one from the fifties that specifically stated Lester Fisher was not originally supposed to be working during the Explosion and that he had traded shifts with a friend.

To follow are clips from the *Halifax Chronicle-Herald*, 1958:

Four Bodies Recovered
Early rescue operations brougnt the bodies of four men to the surface: Lester Fisher, wno was working an extra shift for a friend; Gerald Dawson, Ephraim Alderson and Durrell Pepperdine.

* * *

At the pithead 15 ambulances, scores of private cars, large supplies of medical equipment were in readiness. Some 25 doctors and 40 nurses were also on hand. Offers of help came from all parts of the continent.

The explosion brought with it a crop of stories of freakish circumstances that put some men among the trapped and others, who ordinarily would have been in the mines, safely above the ground.

That's when I set out to find his family, see if I could learn anything from them about who this man was and get the other side of this story.

I posted my desire to talk to someone in his family on a Springhill Facebook page (Blast from Our Past). I wanted to find out if the stories we'd heard were true and find out a bit about this man who was a victim of the Explosion during a shift when he wasn't supposed to be there. Right away, people got me in contact with his daughter, Ethel.

Ethel, indeed, remembered the same story we had always been told. I had my confirmation that

Lester was that person who died in my grandfather's place. I'm very grateful to Lester's daughter, Ethel, for being willing to talk to me (and to Gary Copeland, who connected us. Gary is married to Ethel's cousin, and went to school with my father).

Ironically, it turns out our family is related. Ethel's husband, Bill, was the nephew of my Great Uncle Marvin Megeney. She is also friends with a lot of people in my family. She even has a few items in her home that belonged to my great grandmother, affectionately known throughout Springhill as "Ma McKay."

1. Ethel, tell us about your father. What was he like? What were his interests?

My dad loved to hunt. Hunting season started around October 15th. He liked to hunt anything. Deer. Moose. You could shoot a moose if you found one back then without a permit. He hunted rabbits. He trapped animals like muskrats, beavers, and ducks. He and his friends used to trap them and then go each morning to tend to the traps. They'd skin and stretch them and then sell the fur. That's how they made extra money. Nearly everyone was hunting or fishing for extra money.

Besides hunting and fishing in the winter

time, he had a place off the porch of our house, set up to make flies for fishing. People would come from all over to buy those. Back in those days, people didn't have fishing poles like they do today. We had poles all over our house from his projects.

He also built block walls for people around houses and chimneys. Back in those days, you had to do all sorts of jobs. He kept busy all the time to make extra money. He was a good dad. We never went without anything. We always had everything we ever needed.

He and my mother got married in 1935, and they had two children: myself and my older brother, Art.

2. What was your father's job underground in the mines?

He was a chain runner, working with cars as they would come down into the mines. He went in the mines around 1940. My uncle and his brother, Harold Fisher, also worked for the mines. My father worked during the war. So many miners didn't go to war because the coal had to come up for fuel. He didn't talk a whole lot about his work underground.

3. As you know, one of the reasons I wanted to talk to you was to learn more about this man who ended up dying instead of my grandfather because they swapped shifts with each other. What do you remember about the events before the Explosion and what your father was doing?

My dad would often exchange shifts with another miner. He'd switch to working the afternoon shift, so he could hunt in the morning. He exchanged a lot during hunting season. He just wanted to be out in those woods. He was 43 years old at the time of the Explosion.

The night before the Explosion, it was Halloween. Bill (my fiancé at the time) and I got dressed up and went visiting relatives. (We even went to Bill's grandmother's house, Grandma Megeney, to scare her.) When I came home that night, Mom (Janie Fisher) said she was going out to pick up Dad at work. He was working the night shift that night, too. So I decided to keep my costume on and go with Mom to pick up Dad. So he got to see me in my costume. That night was the last time I'd ever see him. He was off hunting early the next morning.

4. What do you remember about the day of the Explosion? Where were you when it exploded?

I was nineteen years old and teaching in Valley Road. Bill came down to Valley Road and told me there was an explosion. My mom was working at the hospital. When Mom came home, we went out to the mines.

My dad was one of the first to come out of those they found dead in the mines. Of course they were sealed caskets, including for the ones at the top of the mines who were burnt by the Explosion. It was a whirlwind around here.

After the Explosion, Mom was accepted into a school to become a certified nursing assistant.

Map of the mine after the Explosion: (courtesy of the Springhill Miners' Museum)

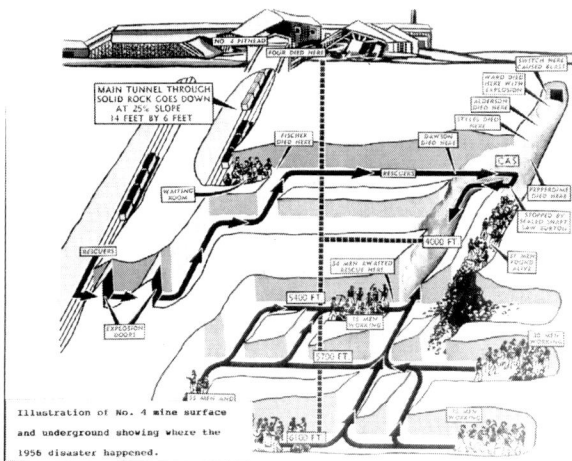

Illustration of No. 4 mine surface and underground showing where the 1956 disaster happened.

Ripple Effect of Life

So, where do you fit into this story?

While my search for this story may have started from the desire to write a screenplay (and novel), what I found was so much bigger.

It's about legacies. It's about what you do with the time you have. It's about how you affect other people.

I think of it like ripples, how when you throw a stone into the water, it tends to ripple out from where it lands, having a far reach.

As small as the town of Springhill is, I want its story to have a far reach and long outlive any of us who had something to do with it — whether we lived through it ourselves or our families lived through it.

As mentioned, I was on a quest to uncover the story behind my grandfather's life being saved from the 1956 Explosion. Yet the sobering part of that story is to know that it also meant the death of someone else. I knew if my grandfather had died that day, I would never have been born. In fact, without death and the multiple tragedies reflected in this story, I wouldn't be here today.

Have you ever pondered the events that brought you to this earth? Have you ever asked yourself the question, "How was I born into my particular family? Why am I here? What was I meant to do?"

The Explosion wasn't the first time my grandfather's life was spared. His first mining accident was in the Springhill mines in the 1940s, and contributed to him not having to go off to war because he suffered a broken pelvis.

As you know, after the Bump in 1958, my father anxiously awaited news of whether or not his dad was still alive, from the Lamp Cabin, a place where miners turned in their lamps when they finished their shifts. His father's check number, #712, remained on the board, showing that he had not yet surfaced. He had not yet picked up his check tag.

Once the earliest miners were rescued, my grandfather was the third person to walk through that Lamp Cabin door. The first face he saw was my dad's fourteen-year-old face, waiting for him, hoping and praying he was still alive.

When "Dado" vowed to never go underground again and he moved the family to Boston, this move is how my father met my mother. When they met, she was an attractive 16-year-old, a spunky Massachusetts girl that he was set up with on a blind date.

Before meeting her, he tried to gamble this blind date away in a poker game, but he had no takers. When she walked through the door, all of those guys wished they had just won her in the "poker pot." Dad was glad he hadn't given her away, after all, and he's never let go of her since. (My parents are close to celebrating 50 years of marriage.)

This blind date never would have happened if my grandfather had not been spared from the 1956 Explosion or survived the 1958 Bump, the tragedy that made him decide to leave his life of mining. My father has said, unequivocally, he would have had no reason to leave Canada had he not been moved to the United States with his father's career change.

My parents have been married since 1966. It's ironic to think that this disaster (and the fact that "Dado's" life was spared from the Explosion 10 years before my parents got married) is the catalyst that brought me to this earth.

At the same time, it's sobering because so many men lost their lives, including the beloved Lester Fisher who just innocently wanted to go hunting that fateful day, November 1, 1956. He was too young to die.

This story helps me connect specific dots that allowed me to enter the scene. It makes me ponder why I am here and encourages me to want to make the most of the life I am given and do at least a little bit of good with whatever days I am blessed to have.

It reminds me of how we are not promised any particular amount of days. I hope those reading this book will be encouraged to make an impact with their lives, no matter how long they are on this earth.

Any ideas for how you'd like to change the world? Your family? Or even just the life of one person? You never know when that may have a ripple effect on the lives of many others.

I also encourage anyone reading this to take the time to gather the stories of your ancestors. Use this time to record them, while they are alive and able to share their stories or those who left this earth before them. Get them down. You just might uncover stories that are worth sharing with the world.

And remember there are miracles that happen all around us. We need to celebrate them, big and small.

Denise, Cheryl, Tom, Heather (2001)

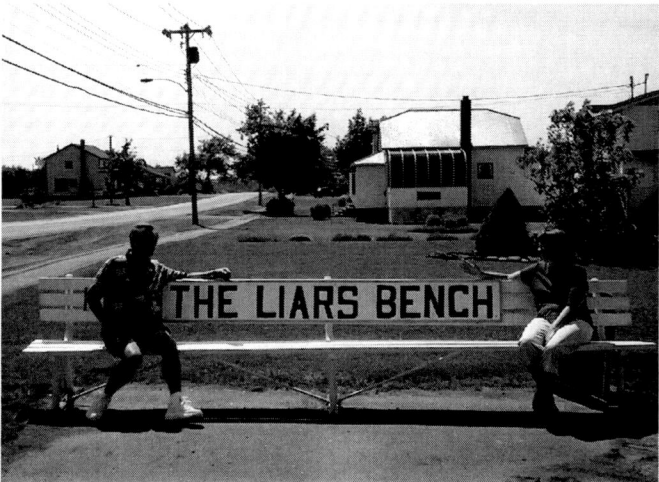

Tom & Denise McKay
Telling "Lies" on the Liar's Bench (2003)

Cheryl & Heather (2001)

**The McKays on the site where the
Springhill Mines used to be (2003)**

Cheryl with Marvin Megeney (2003)

**Cheryl at the Memorial honoring
the 1958 Bump Victims (2003)**

In Loving Memory of
Charles Hugh McKay
March 3, 1915-January 5, 1986
&
Ethel Mae (Tooke) McKay
June 2, 1913-April 18, 1978

Cheryl, Dado, & Nanny (Ethel)

Special Thanks:

To all of those who helped me research this story
or allowed me to interview them, including:

Dad — Tom "Tommy" McKay
Joyce & Gerald Harroun
Caleb & Pat Rushton
Bill Booth
Jerry Gillis
Ken Melanson
Herb Pepperdine
Jack & Keith Bourgeois
Dr. Arnold Burden
Ken Warren
Lloyd Moss
Norma Ruddick
Valerie Ruddick MacDonald
Barry MacDonald
Halifax Chronicle-Herald
Springhill Record
Cumberland Museum
Valarie Tabor Alderson
Gary Copeland
Ethel Fisher Gilbert
Peter Harroun
Debbie Betty-Brazie
Roberta McMasters
Don Tabor
Springhill Heritage Group
Springhill Mine Museum
The Giver of Miracles

Song of Springhill

a love story

an inspirational romance
based on historical events

cheryl mckay

Song of Springhill
a love story

Could you fall in love despite the great risk of losing the one you cherish most?

Hoping for a fresh start, Hannah Wright moves to Springhill, the hometown of the father she never knew because he died in their volatile coal mines before she was born. She tracks down her aunt, Abigail Percy, and is immediately welcomed to move in with the whole Percy clan. This includes her Uncle Ray, a coal miner, and their four lively children. Suddenly, she's surrounded by more family than she's ever had in her life.

The day after she arrives, the mine explodes, trapping many underground, including Uncle Ray. Little did Hannah know when she set off on this new adventure how much her family was going to need her. When the Percys face a sudden lack of provision, Hannah knows she must get a job to help them. But the only industry in town that pays enough is coal mining—and the mine company doesn't hire women.

Hannah secretly masquerades as a man and gets hired as "Mel," a distant cousin of her father's. Keeping up her charade is challenging in this tight-knit, 1950s town, where everybody knows one another.

Hannah is placed on the team of Josh Winslow, a handsome bachelor who noticed her the moment she stepped into town. It doesn't take long for Josh to see through Hannah's disguise as "Mel," but she convinces him there's no other way for her to help take care of her family. Understanding the pressure she's under, he agrees to not blow Hannah's cover — for now.

Though Hannah seems to keep Josh at arm's length, he's determined to chip away at her defenses and win her heart. She resists, afraid to love someone who could die at any moment in an accident underground.

Long-time miners start to sense that "the big one" is coming. Calling it a "Bump" does little to calm Hannah's fear of the impending underground earthquake, a disaster that could come any day.

Will Josh and Hannah be among the next miners caught in a catastrophic disaster? Does Hannah stand to lose everything she's worked so hard to rebuild?

Song of Springhill is a love story set against the backdrop of true-life disasters that plagued the town of Springhill, Nova Scotia in the 1950s. It was a town torn by tragedy that also experienced some of the most astounding, miraculous rescues the world ever watched unfold.

About the Author

Cheryl McKay has been professionally writing since 1997. Tommy Nelson served as her first publisher, teaming her with Frank Peretti on the *Wild and Wacky, Totally True Bible Stories* series. Cheryl wrote the screenplay adaptation of *The Ultimate Gift*, the feature film starring Academy Award Nominees James Garner and Abigail Breslin. It's based on Jim Stovall's best-selling novel. The film was released by Fox in theaters in Spring 2007 and has won such awards as the Crystal Heart Award, the Crystal Dove, one of the Top Ten Family Movies at MovieGuide Awards, and a CAMIE Award. She also wrote the DVD for *Gigi: God's Little Princess*, another book adaptation based on the book by Sheila Walsh. She wrote a half-hour drama for teenagers about high school violence, called *Taylor's Wall*, produced in Los Angeles by Family Theater Productions. After winning a fellowship, she was commissioned to write a feature script, *Greetings from the Flipside,* for Art Within, which Rene Gutteridge and McKay released as a novel through B&H Publishing in October 2013. Her screenplay, *Never the Bride,* was adapted into a novel by Gutteridge and was released by Waterbrook Press in June 2009. The film version is in development. As one passionate for those who are losing hope in their wait to find love, she released the non-fiction version, *Finally the Bride: Finding Hope While Waiting.* She also penned her autobiography, *Finally Fearless: Journey from Panic to Peace.* She wrote the screen story for *The Ultimate Life,* the sequel to *The Ultimate Gift.* Find her on Facebook, Twitter, Pinterest, or at her website, **www.purplepenworks.com** or **www.finallyone.com**.

Books by Cheryl McKay

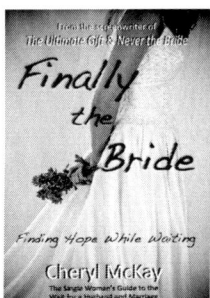
Finally the Bride
Finding Hope While Waiting
Cheryl McKay
From the screenwriter of The Ultimate Gift & Never the Bride
The Single Woman's Guide to the Wait for a Husband and Marriage

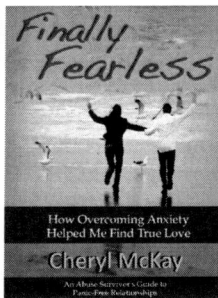
Finally Fearless
How Overcoming Anxiety Helped Me Find True Love
Cheryl McKay
An Abuse Survivor's Guide to Panic-Free Relationships

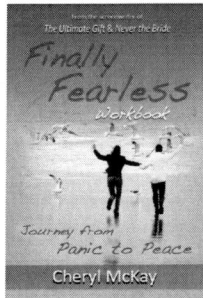
Finally Fearless Workbook
From the screenwriter of The Ultimate Gift & Never the Bride
Journey From Panic to Peace
Cheryl McKay

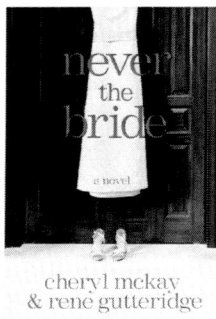
never the bride
a novel
cheryl mckay
& rené gutteridge

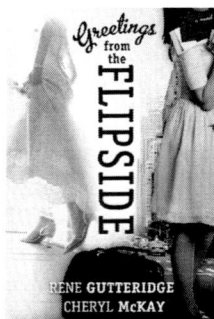
Greetings from the FLIPSIDE
RENE GUTTERIDGE
CHERYL McKAY

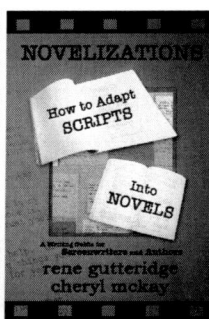
NOVELIZATIONS
How to Adapt SCRIPTS Into NOVELS
A Writing Guide for Screenwriters and Authors
rene gutteridge
cheryl mckay

30614363R00074